To Lynne

[signature]

UNLOCKING INNERMOST THOUGHTS

Andrew Beattie

UNLOCKING INNERMOST THOUGHTS
Copyright © 2022 by Andrew Beattie

ISBN 978-1-915223-08-1

All rights reserved.

No part of this publication may be reproduced, stored in a retrieval system, or transmitted in any form or by any means, electronic, mechanical, photocopying or otherwise, without prior written consent of the publisher except as provided by under United Kingdom copyright law. Short extracts may be used for review purposes with credits given.

Published by
Maurice Wylie Media
Your Inspirational Book Publisher

Based in Northern Ireland and distributing around the world.

www.MauriceWylieMedia.com

Contents

Leonardo	9
An Inspirational Haven	10
Indulging In Satisfaction	11
A Sense of Freedom	12
A Gypsy at Heart	13
Oblivion	14
The Looking Glass	15
Contentment	16
Insignificant	17
The Crisp of Nature	18
A Sense of Purpose	19
Into the Night	20
Rivers of Suggestion	21
Hope	22
Touching on a Gift	23
The Idealism of Consciousness	24
Moments of Doubt	25

Branches of Knowledge	26
Common Sin	27
Contempt of Reality	28
Dreams	29
A Ray of Sunlight	30
Amputate	31
A Bewildering Beauty	32
The Core of Life	33
Drawn	34
This Schizophrenic Weather	35
Castigation	36
Social Awkwardness	37
Inflammatory Insane	38
Suffocation	39
Spiritual Illumination	40
The Demise of Normality	41
The Jaws of Life	42
Dundonald Cemetery	43

Leonardo

I will never comply to a monotonous world
The slaves happily form the conveyor belt
Shattering a fortified youthful ambition
Demanding a sense of worthlessness.

I smell, taste and feel freedom every single moment of life
No one, repeat no-one, will ever take that away from me!
I would love to share my thoughts with like-minded people
Sadly, no-one will ever open their God given mind.

Even though genius is wrapped around my core
Respect does not come from the corruptible and entangled masses
I shrug it off with nonchalant oblivion
For my genuine and compassionate nature will not be disturbed.

Come and let us feast on individuality
Replenish with a gift to the lowest of the low
Deep imagination; dancing with delight
Showering me with natural fulfilment
For I am one of unique breed.

An Inspirational Haven

Particles of dandelion float innocently around my face
Some lie upon the surface of my hair
While others drift aimlessly high above the native trees
Creating a mountain of delight.

The pond a mass of blue
Fishermen cast at their leisure
Baking in the afternoon sunshine with long contented smiles
Giggling school children stand near the waters' edge
Lured by the fresh light ripples.

The delicate sky surreal and beautiful
A private plane flies gently overhead
A flock of birds surge towards a derelict building
That entices from beyond the hill.

Overheated dogs of all shapes and sizes
Marched along by overbearing owners
Toddlers stray from parents reach
Who panic, when out of a moment's sight.

An inspirational haven on one's own doorstep
For people from all walks of life
Soothing many a poor soul
Cradling those of heavy heart.

Indulging in Satisfaction

Twisted trees slouching over river
Cloudy murky water still gleaming
Escaped branches float idly by
Indulging in satisfaction.

Traffic loud and clear
Laughter springs to life
Children scavenge on the bank
Pumped up, military-style.

A stray dog paddles in the water
Tongue hanging and panting for breath
Foaming saliva lingering from its mouth
Still managing a contented smile.

Young woman solemn in thought
Texting frantically on her phone
She plucks the wild flowers
Then looks to the sky for guidance.

An elderly man passes by saying, "Hello," in my direction
I return the word with a fresh smile
The dusk is starting to fall
I leave quietly with an unassuming manner.

A Sense of Freedom

Hailstones pound upon the garden
Nature creates havoc
Rose bush flaps intensely
A bed of ice protrudes
Beside the battered gate.

Leaping over the fence
Bouncing frantically
With a clacking sound
Quickly becoming soggy underfoot.

Sky covered in darkness
Water leaks from loose rooftop spout
Ice particles stranded on derelict walls
Doors and windows firmly closed.

Children run for home from school
Pandemonium reigns in the air
School bags come to their aid
Providing temporary shelter.

Something mysterious about the elements
How they dance freely
The one in Heaven laughs
Let the world walk on by.

A Gypsy at Heart

I was born with self-destruct
The bizarre madness will gladly conduct
Listening to moonshine words in every melancholy bar
Sleeping; under a disconnected star.

The masses sharpen their knives, I'm ready for ridicule
End of another disastrous evening, idiotic fool
Jaundiced atmosphere
I quickly depart
Walking unconcerned
A gypsy at heart.

Concentrated quietism unshackles, leaving me free to roam
Boastful testosterone
Guaranteed to find a temporary home
Nature of the beast; no-one specifically to blame
Dubious in the morning
Undoubtedly with no shame.

Oblivion

The rain falls in straight lines
As vulnerability clings
Taste for life is slipping away
Inability to cope
The mind never runs smooth.

Echo of madness swirls
I catch my breath
Passing corridors of emptiness
Falling; into an abyss.

Under volcanic rock
Into depths of the unknown
Drowning in an ocean of anguish
Unobtrusively, into unconsciousness.

I left the working world at seventeen
Already bored with mainstream society
Humiliation seeps into a misjudged wound
Lying motionless in a bed of self-pity.

The Looking Glass

I struggle with half a smile through bitterness
The clown laughs away an April shower of tears
Alcohol does its best to dull lively senses
At least helpful when trying to unwind.

This place alive with vitality and youthfulness
Louder than the echoes of manic children
Fruit machines light up the evening air
As droves of people rush happily by.

I stray in my mind where I am safe
To conjure beautiful, poetical visions
Gazing beyond the spirituality of stars
Which captivate long into the still night.

Ah, the purest of love
Exists inside a delicate soul
Analysed through the looking glass
Which bites every known hand that feeds.

A regret falls from ashen face
Middle age sneakily creeps up and agitates
The looking glass fails to tell the whole story
Oh how the mind
Never lies.

Contentment

A gentle flowing stream trickles
Nonchalantly through common terrain
Scattered dead leaves
Amongst winter withered grass
November frost bites down sharply on icicle hands
However the mind smiles abundantly
With opportunity and optimism.

Standing tall in admiration
And only a stone's throw away
A loyal benevolent surge
To be reckoned with
Shimmering waters
Darkness ready to fall
Contentment stands firm with adorable fulfilment.

Unlocking the doors to my innermost thoughts
And poetically woven mind,
Interact and entwine into a gift of natural beauty
Oozing with a joyous, bountiful belief
Inspirational dreams undoubtedly await to entice.

Insignificant

Tissue of conceit
Pours from shameless cloud
Agitating sky chastises
The severity of loneliness.

Laughter of fools
Disturbs the solitude
Social anxiety prevails
For which no antidote.

A segment of fulfilment
Quickly swept aside
Insignificant
Sterile boredom takes hold.

The seed of disenchantment
Has been sown.

The Crisp of Nature

End of March devours
With colder, bluer days
Clouds angry from bitter, biting winds
At a loose end,
Will it ever disappear?
Alas, I concede
Gracious in defeat.

Harsh winter eats like cancer
Thoughts of pessimism come to the fore
Snowbound days sticking with frustration
People struggling to and fro.

Let Spring push forward with optimism
Long and warm
Shimmering bright nights
Shaking dust from one's feet
And the weariness of the world.

Hanging on for taste of summer
Delicious golden rays tanning toned skin
Igniting a passion that lay dormant for centuries
The crisp of nature
Let it burn with desire.

A Sense of Purpose

I just opened a strong beer beside an overpowering tree
Sun burning like mad onto delicate Irish skin
I am looking straight ahead at an ancient ruin
Created by Augustus
To rival his great uncle Julius.

I am totally surrounded by ancient Roman history
How the mind wonders and ponders
To dictators, power and greed
What has changed since then?
Absolutely nothing.

I sit on a sturdy bench and open another beer
Now I am surrounded by loud, soft and whispering voices
Also a cluster of in depth and studious people
Where is the stirring of irrational behaviour?
Buried beneath the rubble, yearning for the past.

I may burn under the Roman sun
Still it is better than a face-full of Belfast rain
Where the cold gnaws your very fibre
More so in the dead of winter.

I wish I could step back in time
To grasp that feeling of the ancient Roman era
To taste the madness of Nero, Julius,
Augustus, Caligula et cetera.
To touch upon early poets
Virgil, Ovid and Horace to name a few
Ah, at least I am here
To capture a sense of purpose.

Into the Night

Into the night
Long, long into the night
I dread the loss of Heaven
I fear the pit of Hell.

Alone and lost in thought
The gnawing pain in my stomach
Disproportionate levels of anxiety
Destroying functional ability.

Into the night
Long, long into the night.

Languishing in the bowels of obscurity
Whilst the body yearns to exist
The mind wanders to a far-off corner
Soul-searching for hidden utopianism.

Into the night
Long, long into the night.

I do not rejoice or sit in comfort
Watching the thickening doors
Demanding closure
Probing the grey and white matter of the brain
Subduing the essence of reality.

Into the night
Long, long, long into the night.

Rivers of Suggestion

Fascinated by rivers of suggestion
A visualisation of fresh ambition
Emerging from perfectly formed sincerity
Reflecting through eyes of honesty.

Holding optimism in healing hands
Challenged by sneering pessimism
Which I defiantly shrug off
Laughter fills luminous mountainside
Dismantling ambiguity
Expressing clarity with boldness.

Hope

When the darkness appears there is light
Through hopelessness there is hope
When sadness looms over our world
A great strength can spring from nowhere
Bringing a steely determination.

Through life's ills we can find an open door
Where hope can touch our weakness
The power of a strong inner belief
Stretching as far as the heavenly realms.

Optimism flourishes when we least expect
Even in a desperate place
Where the soul is purified
Through the water of life
Yes, there is hope in all that we do
Achievement can come in many different forms
We just have to open our eyes and believe.

Touching on a Gift

My law of gravity has no ending
Finding a haven in spiritual dimension
Soaring supersonic to the path of nirvana
Earthly death thrusting the eagerness of immortality.

The great beyond awaits
Supernova transcends before my very eyes
A spellbinding luminous warmth decorates the passing of sky
Transporting through time
Offering infinity.

Expanding organic organism
Reaching out in faith
Floating through the universe on angelic plane
Where no human form can taste.

Touching on a gift
Sucking your intellect
Stars close by
Heaven just a whisper.

The Idealism of Consciousness

Oh perfect sleep and rest
Dull the senses evermore
Natural earthly soil, let me taste
Cover my lifeless brow, I command.

To have no more worldly pain
Never again to suffer at the hand of fools
Loneliness and isolation finally gone
Aging skin and weary eyes disintegrate.

What really happens in the afterlife? Is there an afterlife?
I want to know right now!
A beautiful new beginning, maybe
The idealism of consciousness.

Do I want to leave this mortal coil? Do I?
Never to feel the warmth of a lady
Or my arrogance every again
Never to ponder, wonder or dream
Well do I?

Do I yearn for these things?
Do I? No!
The mere thought of living forever
That in itself is frightening
I think.

Moments of Doubt

Always blessed with great imagination
Moments of doubt
Lacking formal education
The complexity of word struggling to pronounce
How pathetic
How absurd.

Feeling inadequate when facing intellect
To make a feeble excuse
Then vanish into thin air
Nothing but relentless suffocation
Drowning in awkward conversation.

Branches of Knowledge

Enduring gracefully a touch of autism
Which seeps from the brain
Isolating reality
Opening the floodgates to branches of knowledge
And inner purity.
Treading diligently when analysing my recent past
The curse of the overactive mind
Still overflowing with poetical abundance.

Treating me with disdain
Whilst I barely exist
Surrounded by dilapidated structures still smiling deep within
My playful defence mechanism.
An Oxford dictionary comforts and soothes on long, lonely nights
The perfect worldly Bible which frees me from insanity
Stirring the foundation of intellect.

Unambiguous train of thought teases the disheartening jungle
The disciplined antidote which dispels a heavy burden
Nature is a language that replenishes the soul
Open your eyes to exhume its buried treasure.

Common Sin

How the envy runs into the night
Where there is dim candlelight
And how the soul burns with rage
So frequently with a mere turn of a page.

It eats until there is nothing left within
Oh, such a pathetic but common sin
Now there's only flat and warm beer
My friend, for the likes of you
The end draws mightily near.

Contempt of Reality

I am mortified for my whole life has been
Tediously excruciating
Seeking shelter in a cold and lonely bed
The heart spurts onto unsympathetic floor
Brain vegetating, exposed and scattered
Without compassion.

Aspirations are long gone
Nothing left
A confused head now buried in enticing sand
The easy escape route when disaster strikes
I will be judged unreasonably for my contempt of reality.

Far beneath the indestructible surface lies a glimmer of hope
Ready to shake the foundation of normality and acceptance
A stubborn defiant streak that will not slip quietly by
Pride that I inherited from my noble and ancestral seat.

Dreams

Never laugh at anyone's dreams
For a person without dreams has nothing
Yes! The world will laugh and scorn
Pouring contempt upon a delicate head.
Oh, you are different from most of the human race
A childlike innocence with so much soul
Suffering in silence day in and day out
Overwhelmed by loneliness many a time.
Uniqueness seeks transformation, a dance of delight
To touch a mind and give hope
Leaving beauty embedded forevermore
So reach for the heavens and find your ultimate goal.

A Ray of Sunlight

A ray of sunlight radiates through grim reality
Of modern-day commercialism
Breathing, which leaves a shimmering taste of transparency
Entering profoundly and extracting
A great wealth of literary knowledge
Cherishing every iconic moment on this ocean of euphoria.

A ray of sunlight regenerates life into my idealistic safe haven
Even though November is the gloomiest month of all
Some gentle warmth for homo-sapiens to acknowledge
At last, to soak in sublime fulfilment.

Amputate

A waft of clemency
Consoles the pilgrim
Fortune favours the brave
Whilst faint-hearted despair.

Redemption in virgin territory
Lost through dense fern
Falling into the unknown
Transparency reflects kindly.

I clasp for affection
Finding nourishment in your lap
Relaxing in dappled grass
Succumb to natural instinct.

Feeding eroticism expands a moreish thought
Clock is ticking
Confiscate audacity
Amputate the scholarly mind.

A Bewildering Beauty

Out of tragic circumstances
That disturb the very foundation
A bewildering beauty can be born
At times it is hard to fathom
When holding head in hands
And weeping with anguish.

Laughter, happiness and love
Already a distant memory
From the recent past
With a sense of innocent purity
Can once again be found.
Believing wholeheartedly that one will find a key
To unlock the door to purpose in life
Even though sibling rivalry
And fair-weather friends try your patience
A deaf ear tingles with many obtuse words.

It will take more than sexual gratification
To inspire
When lost and deep in thought
A bewildering beauty can spring from dire
Sodden clay
Shake off the cloud of obscurity
Rise like a phoenix
From the ashes.

The Core of Life

To hate with darkened passion
Submerging into my interior being
When the core of life goes disastrously wrong
Why is the world full of stereotypical bores?
Machine like robots marching as one
Clueless, gutless and soulless.
Why? Why? Why?

Drawn

Trees in the moonlight make me quiver
Particularly through the still of night
Enchanting castle sits proudly in the foreground
The sleeping Cavehill lies in the background.

I feel drawn into your presence
Muddy slopes beckon to test endurance
Where time stops for everyone
I believe
For poet, clerk, labourer, genius or fool.

This Schizophrenic Weather

Through light then heavy showers
All she ever wanted
Was a bouquet of flowers
This schizophrenic weather would confuse
Any mortal man
Strewn along the weary ground
Lay many an empty beer can.

Golden silence
No need for deafening word
The very thought
So absurd
Just the taste of tranquillity
With added bliss
That comes from simplicity
And a tender loving kiss.

Castigation

Poetic words summoned to the front of imaginative mind
Senses sharpen through tedious daily grind
Dreams vast like oceans
Merging into a must need
Ingenious thoughts migrate from a nothing seed.

To step back in time
Castigation made me flee
Finding solitude under the grand sycamore tree
Enlightened by thunderstorms
Which brought mass whipping winds
And biblical rain
Seclusion can be testing
The aggravation from a lonely pain.

Social Awkwardness

Humiliation has left the senses feeling painfully shy
They want to flee and simply die
Terrified and covered in stupidity
It's absolutely vile
I could run a country mile.

Social awkwardness affects my overactive brain
I keep thinking that I'm going insane
Truly a heart-rending ill
For me the usual
Bland
Run of the mill.

So many difficult decisions
Most definitely have to be made
When insecurity takes hold
I just want to fade
The lack of communication
Sinking to the depths of despair
Longing for something
Or someone to share.

Inflammatory Insane

Catching the visions of the night
Through unrelenting black rain
Feeling disturbed and disorientated
With nothing to gain.
Streetlights fascinate
Guiding unrepentantly through witching hour
Shimmering whilst reflecting
Unexpectedly upon shabby car.

Uncultivated head unconscious
Contented upon soft feather pillow
Right through the ugly, gloomy night
Except for me
Fighting back with all my might.
The eerie, mesmeric silence
Could be broken
By the slightest thing
Insomnia through loneliness
Through barbarism castrates
Leaving a deadly sting.

January guaranteed to be an achingly heart-wrenching time
Delicately frustrating when in angelic prime
The morning forecast is for more black rain.
Mind playing tricks
Inflammatory insane
More, more, more constant black rain.

Suffocation

Why do we all have to die someday?
Filling me with horrific and dreadful fear
Too brutally honest for my own good
I tell you no word of a lie.

To shed a ghastly tear
The bewildering storm is upon us
Loose gate rattling until the morning light
Only then, does my suffocation end.

Spiritual Illumination

When desperation takes hold we see only the darkness
The arousing of bitter indignation
Only leads to complication
To fortify is to breed steely determination
A cry of joy to push the boundaries.

Dancing when skies are grey
To smile in the face of adversary
The act of individualism will not tarnish
Nor be forsaken.

Let spiritual illumination arise
Go forth and multiply
The law of nature stands at the door
Enticing with a bountiful gift.

The Demise of Normality

Cold biting winds eat away at my discontented mind
And dishevelled appearance
Unkempt hair
A putrid odour defines the body
The lack of vital nourishment leaves me shrivelled from neglect
Scaly patches on face
Blood shot eyes
Terrified and soulless
Pathetic lips covered with weeping cold sores
A scraggy beard that festers
Unembarrassed.

Clothes which are torn and shabby through harsh conditions
The nature of reality testing the most vulnerable
A condemned soul
Unloved, Unemployable
And in deep despair
Ostracised unfairly by society in general
A hopeless pessimism devours the very flesh.

The Jaws of Life

I walk home alone
With laboured breath
Having given everything to Caesar
Abstaining from the tempting clutches of alcohol
Criticised for sobriety by the blood thirsty masses
The demonic consequences are far too great to comprehend.

Negative thoughts come easily in the morning
Long after the poisonous liquid
had entered the gullet with anticipation
The muscular organ that pumps life around the body
Flowed generously with excitement
Preying on a vulnerable nature.

I found refuge through escapism
To be ambitious in a dream
My arms stretched out
Reaching for the jaws of life
Waiting patiently to be romantically challenged
The reality of life has taken its toll.

The quill is eagerly awaiting
Musing over yesterday's hero with feet of clay
Divulging my individuality throughout the universe
For a prophet is not accepted in his home town.

Dundonald Cemetery

Walking through the quaint village of Dundonald
The seventy mile an hour wind plays havoc
With my body and thoughts
Heavy rain falls upon my weary and now saturated head
I struggle immensely to keep my composure
In these atrocious conditions.

The nearby trees twist, turn and threaten
To crash down onto the narrow road
Vehicles tightly parked
Functioning at a snail's pace
Drivers full of anger and frustration
Concerned by the lack of progress through the village.

I finally arrive at my destination
Dundonald Cemetery
Poignantly reading the names, birth dates
And hour of death on so many headstones
Looking for my grandparents' grave
Was similar to an exploration
There was no headstone nor simple plaque of identification
My uncle's baby son and my aunt
Also sleep peacefully in the same unmarked grave.

Oh, so many lives, where are they all now?
Born into this world then sadly disappear without a trace
Passionate belief triggered by the echoes of resistance
Now they are gone
On a path to another dimension.

Contact the Author by emailing

AndrewBeattiePoetry@gmail.com

INSPIRED TO WRITE A BOOK?

Contact
Maurice Wylie Media
Your Inspirational Book Publisher

Based in Northern Ireland and distributing around the world.
www.MauriceWylieMedia.com